Let's Talk:
Sharing Our Thoughts and Feelings During Times of Crisis

FOCUS ON FAMILY MATTERS

Focus on Family Matters

Let's Talk:
Sharing Our Thoughts and Feelings During Times of Crisis

Michele Alpern

Marvin Rosen, Ph.D.
Consulting Editor

CHELSEA HOUSE
P U B L I S H E R S
A Haights Cross Communications Company
Philadelphia

CHELSEA HOUSE PUBLISHERS

EDITOR IN CHIEF Sally Cheney
DIRECTOR OF PRODUCTION Kim Shinners
CREATIVE MANAGER Takeshi Takahashi
MANUFACTURING MANAGER Diann Grasse

Staff for LET'S TALK: SHARING OUR THOUGHTS AND FEELINGS DURING TIMES OF CRISIS

ASSOCIATE EDITOR Bill Conn
PICTURE RESEARCHER Sarah Bloom
PRODUCTION ASSISTANT Jaimie Winkler
COVER AND SERIES DESIGNER Takeshi Takahashi
LAYOUT 21st Century Publishing and Communications, Inc.

A Haights Cross Communications ✦ Company

http://www.chelseahouse.com

First Printing

1 3 5 7 9 8 6 4 2

Library of Congress Cataloging-in-Publication Data

Alpern, Michele.
  Let's talk : sharing our thoughts and feelings during times of crisis / Michele Alpern.
    p. cm.—(Focus on family matters)
Includes bibliographical references and index.
  ISBN 0-7910-6954-0
  1. Emotional problems of children—Juvenile literature. [1. Emotional problems.]
I. Title. II. Series.
BF723.E598 A57 2002
155.4'18—dc21

                                                                    2002007868

Contents

Introduction

Marvin Rosen, Ph.D.
Consulting Editor

B ad things sometimes happen to good people. We've probably all heard that expression. But what happens when the
"good people" are teenagers?

Growing up is stressful and difficult to negotiate. Teenagers
are struggling to becoming independent, trying to cut ties with
their families that they see as restrictive, burdensome, and
unfair. Rather than attempting to connect in new ways with
their parents, they may withdraw. When bad things do happen,
this separation may make the teen feel alone in coping with
difficult and stressful issues.

Focus on Family Matters provides teens with practical information about how to cope when bad things happen to them.
The series deals foremost with feelings—the emotional pain
associated with adversity. Grieving, fear, anger, stress, guilt,
and sadness are addressed head on. Teens will gain valuable
insight and advice about dealing with their feelings, and for
seeking help when they cannot help themselves.

The authors in this series identify some of the more serious
problems teens face. In so doing, they make three assumptions:
First, teens who find themselves in difficult situations are not at
fault and should not blame themselves. Second, teens can overcome difficult situations, but may need help to do so. Third,
teens bond with their families, and the strength of this bond
influences their ability to handle difficult situations.

These books are also about communication—specifically
about the value of communication. None of the problems
covered occurs in a vacuum, and none of the situations should

be faced by anyone alone. Each either involves a close family member or affects the entire family. Since families teach teens how to trust, relate to others, and solve problems, teens need to bond with families to develop normally and become emotionally whole. Success in dealing with adversity depends not only on the strength of the individual teen, but also upon the resources of the family in providing support, advice, and material assistance. Strong attachment to care givers in a supporting, nurturing, safe family structure is essential to successful coping.

Some teens learn to cope with adversity—they absorb the pain, they adjust, and they go on. But for others, the trauma they experience seems like an insurmountable challenge—they become angry, stressed, and depressed. They may withdraw from friends, they may stop going to school, and their grades may slip. They may draw negative attention to themselves and express their pain and fear by rebelling. Yet, in each case, healing can occur.

The teens who cope well with adversity, who are able to put the past behind them and regain their momentum, are no less sensitive or caring than those who suffer most. Yet there is a difference. Teens who are more resilient to trauma are able to dig deep down into their own resources, to find strength in their families and in their own skills, accomplishments, goals, aspirations, and values. They are able to find reasons for optimism and to feel confidence in their capabilities. This series recognizes the effectiveness of these strategies, and presents problem-solving skills that every teen can use.

Focus on Family Matters is positive, optimistic, and supportive. It gives teens hope and reinforces the power of their own efforts to handle adversity. And most importantly, it shows teens that while they cannot undo the bad things that have happen, they have the power to shape their own futures and flourish as healthy, productive adults.

Crises

■ Nick clearly remembers the day that his parents announced they were getting a divorce—they were eating dinner when his father said that they needed to discuss something important. The news shouldn't have been such a shock to him, as his parents fought constantly and Nick's dad often slept at a hotel after really bad arguments. But Nick couldn't help but feel like he had been punched in the stomach when he heard his father say, "Your mother and I have decided that the best thing we can do for the family is to get a divorce." Nick wondered how tearing apart the family could possibly be the best thing for them. Nick was angry, and felt like he couldn't tell anyone how he was feeling.

A **crisis** is a situation that is very stressful and disruptive. All of us have experienced stress in daily life—an argument with a friend or family member, a tough test at school, a rough day on the sports field—but we usually find ways to recover from these types of stress and feel better

Anyone can feel overwhelmed by the stress and anxiety that accompany a crisis. There are ways to help resolve these feelings, like taking comfort in the support your loved ones can provide.

quickly. Sometimes, however, situations can be so upsetting that our coping abilities are overwhelmed. At some point or other in our lives, we may find ourselves experiencing a time of such pain, distress, or instability that we are thrown off balance and have a hard time regaining our footing.

It is important for each of us to realize when we are experiencing a crisis and to recognize how we are thinking and feeling during that difficult time, so we can help ourselves heal. Understanding and gaining perspective on upsetting thoughts and feelings helps to make them less confusing, less overwhelming, and easier to resolve.

This book explains the common thoughts and feelings

that crises bring. In addition, it offers specific guidance on how to cope with a crisis, including how to seek assistance from others. Learning about times of distress will help you handle them when they come up in your own life, as well as help you understand and support others when they go through tough times.

Types of crises

Particular situations may bring some of us more distress than others, depending on our unique personalities and life circumstances. For example, the death of a relative is very hard to deal with if the relative was close to you, but it is usually not as rough on you if it was someone you rarely saw. Although our responses to events vary, the following are situations that almost everyone would consider to be a crisis. We will discuss these situations, and some of the common concerns and responses they generate, in the following sections:

Can you describe a crisis you experienced recently? How did you feel?

Severe Illness or Injury—An illness or injury that seriously disrupts your ability to function brings with it tough emotions, including **anxiety**, **grief**, disappointment, anger, and uncertainty. The major illness or injury of someone close to you may be equally stressful.

Death of a Loved One—Although death inevitably comes to all living beings, the pain of losing someone close to you is nonetheless one of the very hardest things to bear. A crisis over the loss commonly follows the death of a close relative, friend, or even pet. Many of us first witness death when a pet passes away.

Major Family Conflict—Parents' divorce is a major source of stress and disruption for children. It also results in the loss of one parent's presence in the household. An even

If you are dealing with a crisis that involves your family, such as a parent's substance abuse or violent behavior, you may have to seek help from another trusted adult like a teacher or a school counselor. Making your concerns known may allow your family to get the help it needs.

more serious problem, all too commonplace, is violence within the family. Family violence may include acts of physical harm or psychological abuse toward a spouse or child, sexual behavior toward a child, or severe neglect of a child. Another serious family problem is drug or alcohol abuse by a parent. Drug and alcohol abuse typically results in irresponsible behavior, an inability to manage daily life, and great mood swings—effects that are deeply stressful to the entire household. If you live in a household in which there is violence or substance abuse, be sure to get help from other adults. You are living in an unsafe environment that is too difficult to manage on your own.

Crime—Victims of crime suffer emotional wounds that are often as painful as physical ones. Examples of crimes that teens may experience are physical assault, rape, robbery, and vandalism. Like family violence, being raped is one of the most emotionally disturbing events anyone, may face.

Natural Disaster—Fires, floods, earthquakes, tornadoes, and hurricanes are very stressful to experience. They may threaten your physical safety, damage your house and possessions, and disrupt your entire community, resulting in serious emotional challenges. Studies have shown that many young people suffer depression and anxiety after a serious natural disaster, even as much as a year after the disaster.

Man-made Disaster—Survivors of a plane crash, bombing, building explosion, terrorist incident, or riot face serious emotional challenges —just as the survivors of a natural disaster do. People who live through a man-made disaster may find the event especially hard to comprehend. They may feel particular anxiety because the event occurred without warning, or may have been deliberate.

How did you feel when you heard about the terrorist attacks on September 11th?

Witnessing a Crisis—People who have merely seen a very stressful event or who have a close relationship with a victim may also suffer feelings typical of a crisis, even though they haven't directly experienced the incident themselves. This phenomenon is important to understand, because we are all exposed to media coverage of crisis events.

For example, the terrorist attacks of September 11, 2001, and the war that followed them were covered around the clock on TV, radio, the Internet, and in newspapers. Watching and hearing reports of such disastrous and unstable events led many people to feel very anxious, sad, and angry—including people who were not directly affected. We need to recognize that events that may not touch us directly may still touch us deeply. It is important to be informed about our world, but we also need to pay attention to our feelings and concerns, and take steps to cope with them the same way we would after a stressful event that we experienced ourselves.

Mental Health Problem—Besides stressful events like disasters, crime, death, illness, and family conflict, problems with our own mental health can also bring about feelings of crisis, especially if they are untreated. Suffering with a mental health condition like **depression** or an anxiety disorder can be just as distressing and disruptive as experiencing a crisis event in the outside world. Sometimes mental health problems are triggered by stressful events like loss, assault, or disaster, and sometimes they occur without any immediate trigger. Chapter 3 of this book focuses particularly on mental health disorders.

Special problems for young adults

Crises are especially difficult for teens because they generally do not have as much experience with the world, and practice with coping skills, as adults do. In addition, the time from about age twelve to age eighteen brings unique challenges. Teens who experience a crisis face its difficulties while they are already coping with the special stresses of growing up.

The teen years are a time of many changes—changes that are normal and positive, but stressful nonetheless. Any

Experiencing a crisis as a teenager can be especially difficult, since you will already be dealing with changes like increased responsibility and maturity. Talking about your feelings with your friends can help, but knowing when to seek help from an adult is essential.

change is stressful, even a good change. Your body is rapidly maturing and you are developing sexually. Teens often begin to experience the confusion and turmoil, as well as the excitement and pleasure, of dating, and may go through relationship break-ups as they begin to sort out what they want in a romantic partner.

Further, during the teen years you gain independence. You come to rely less on your parents and teachers to make decisions and judgments, and more on yourself and your peers. You gain responsibilities in school, like choosing what classes to take, and at home, like being responsible for more household chores. Many teens also get part-time jobs, and many begin to look ahead toward their careers. Teens commonly also begin to drive, acquiring more freedom to go where they want. Becoming more grown-up and independent from your parents is exciting, but it can also be stressful. You may struggle with self-confidence, and you may have conflicts with your parents about making your own decisions.

The normal changes of adolescence can be tough to sort out, but teens usually manage to cope with them well. However, a crisis—a severely disruptive, stressful event or mental health condition—can be uniquely hard to handle when you are already experiencing normal teenage pressures. Further, a serious crisis within the family— such as divorce, family violence, or a parent's substance abuse—is very difficult for teens since they rely on their parents to take care of them. Even though teenagers grow more independent, they still need their parents' emotional and practical support.

Teens in abusive families must seek support from others, like a counselor, teacher, or religious cleric. Teens who are not in abusive families should consider turning to their families for support in a crisis, as well as turning to others; make the most of your parents' experience, maturity, and resources, and their ability and desire to help you. In a crisis, we all need help. This book can offer you information and guidance about times of great stress, enabling you to gain more perspective and cope more easily. It is also important that you communicate your thoughts and feelings with people you trust, to get the support you need.

Common Thoughts and Feelings in Times of Crisis

One night David was on his way to catch a bus home after visiting some friends in another neighborhood. As he headed to the bus stop, a group of older boys stopped in his path and began making fun of him. He tried to walk away but they beat him up, leaving him with a chipped tooth, a black eye, and a lot of bad bruises.

Weeks later, David continues to relive that night. He keeps wondering if he could have done something to prevent getting beaten up. He's jumpy around other kids, especially those he doesn't know well. He's so anxious that he has trouble concentrating in class, and he doesn't sleep well at night. He's embarrassed to let anyone know what's happening with him, so more and more he keeps to himself.

Our feelings and thoughts following a stressful event can be very tough to resolve. Have you ever awakened from a nightmare and felt for a moment that the dream really happened? You probably reminded yourself that it was just a dream and put

The thoughts and emotions you experience after a crisis may leave you feeling alone. It is important to remember that your emotional responses to a crisis are normal, and people who have experienced similar crises feel just like you do.

it behind you. A crisis event, an event that causes great distress and disruption, feels like a nightmare that really *is* happening. And the feelings it creates don't just go away after the incident is over. It can take weeks, months, or sometimes even years to heal fully from the stress.

It is important to recognize the typical emotions and thoughts that crisis events bring. When you understand common responses to crisis events, you can make sense of your own response more easily. You can realize that your reaction is normal, helping you to feel less alone, confused, and embarrassed. When you can sort out and identify your feelings and thoughts, you are better equipped to cope with them.

Fight or flight

When human beings face stress, we undergo what is called a **fight or flight response**. This response has evolved over millions of years and is built into human biology. When our prehistoric ancestors encountered dangers, like an attacking animal or a sudden, violent storm, they had no time to think about how to respond; they had to take immediate action to defend themselves or to run away, in order to stay alive. Their bodies automatically reacted to danger in a way that prepared them to fight or run. Humans still have this bodily reaction to stressful situations, even situations that are not a matter of life or death.

When we face a very stressful situation, our bodies surge with natural chemicals that prepare the body to fight or flee. The heart beats fast, and breathing becomes rapid and shallow. Blood rushes to the muscles, making them tense up. The stomach clenches. The body sweats. The pupils in the eyes grow larger. The mind is quickened. Natural pain killers, called endorphins, numb us to physical pain and to our emotions; in a fight or flight reaction, our bodies do not give us the time to grapple with our feelings. We may feel strangely detached, as though we were in a movie. The body feels like a ringing alarm bell.

> **Can you describe**
>
> **how the fight or flight mechanism might help you in an emergency?**

After a stressful event

What happens to your body after the stressful event concludes? At first, as your fight or flight response fades away, you feel exhausted. The fight or flight response takes a lot out of you. Your energy is so depleted that you may feel depressed. But usually in time your body's chemistry returns to normal.

If the stress was very severe, however, the body's chemical changes may last for a long time. A serious crisis event is hard for the mind to resolve, and as long as you feel that the crisis is unresolved, you will continue to experience the chemical effects of stress. Every time you recall or worry about the incident, your body may go through the fight or flight reaction all over again.

How long and how strongly a stressful event affects you depends on several factors. First, it depends on how long and how intense the event was. Getting a low test grade brings about some stress, but having a serious car accident affects you much more. Some crisis situations, like family violence, last for years and include repeated traumatic incidents; crisis events that go on for an extended period of time are among the very hardest to endure and resolve.

Second, you are generally affected by stress more when the crisis is unpredictable. Hurricanes are usually predicted days, even weeks, in advance, while terrorist bombings may occur without warning. One of the hardest things for people after the September 11th terrorist attack was that they never expected such an incident. They were thoroughly unprepared emotionally, and were uncertain about whether more terrorist acts might follow.

Further, the effects of a stressful event are greater and longer lasting when you bury your feelings about it afterward than when you air your emotions and get support from others. This is very important to note. Ignoring or hiding your feelings about a crisis keeps you from resolving them, and thus prolongs and intensifies them. Instead, addressing the event, talking about it, and turning to others for encouragement and compassion helps you get past the crisis, enabling your body chemistry, your mind, and your emotions to return to normal.

Feelings in times of crisis

We each feel somewhat differently following a crisis event, depending on our personal history, body chemistry, and personality, as well as on the length and intensity of the crisis and our resources of support. If you have faced a stressful event along with other people, you may find that some of them seem to be coping more easily than you are. Remember that they may, in fact, be experiencing greater difficulties than you know, and that there is no single, normal way to feel after a distressing event. Unless your response to the event seriously interferes with your ability to function in daily life for a long time (at least a month), be assured that your reaction is normal. It may take months to feel really healed.

Although stressful events affect each of us differently to some extent, there are a number of common feelings that people have following a crisis. First, the crisis affects the body. Common physical effects include trouble sleeping, problems with appetite, intense fatigue, muscle pains, stomachaches, headaches, and skin rashes.

Second, tough emotions follow a crisis event. Typical emotional reactions include sadness, anger, anxiety, and feelings of helplessness. These feelings can be very intense, but they are natural to have for a time.

Feelings of guilt are also common and can be especially confusing. For example, survivors of a disaster often feel guilty that they fared better than others who were killed or injured. They may question whether they deserved to survive, although the tragic event had nothing to do with the victims' value as people.

How would you feel

if you survived a natural or man-made disaster, but someone close to you did not?

Further, teens whose parents have problems like divorce, family violence, or substance abuse often feel responsible for their parents' behavior. Teens often believe they are to blame, although in fact children cannot cause their parents to divorce or behave abusively; their parents' problems are their own, and have nothing to do with the children's behavior.

Another confusing emotion after a crisis event is feeling very anxious about possible dangers. Having experienced one highly disturbing situation, people often feel that other threats lie everywhere around them. For instance, after someone you love dies, you may feel frightened that you may lose other people. Or if you survived a dangerous event, you may jump out of your seat every time you hear a loud noise, or fear strangers that pass you on the street. The body and mind

A crisis may affect you both physically and emotionally. The stress that follows may cause you to have headaches, stomachaches, and trouble sleeping, as well as strong emotions like anxiety and sadness.

remain keyed up from the stress of the crisis event, so it is normal for a time to feel unusually alert to danger.

Facing all of these tough feelings after a crisis event, people commonly find that they are unable to cope well with the typical stresses of daily life. Their coping abilities have been so strained that any daily problems—a traffic jam, a tough class assignment, a disagreement with a sibling—may seem a lot harder than usual. Be assured that this is also normal.

Numbness

The poet Emily Dickinson wrote, "After great pain, a formal feeling comes." She likened the aftereffects of a painful event to coming inside after being frozen in the snow: "First—Chill—then Stupor—then the letting go." The first reaction to a very disturbing situation is commonly shock and disbelief. As noted previously, the fight or flight response numbs your emotions, making you feel disconnected from events. For some people, especially teenagers, this "chill" stage lingers for a considerable time, making it hard to achieve the "letting go."

Following a crisis, many teens try to appear as though nothing serious has happened. Often they hide their feelings about the event, even to themselves. They may try to avoid thinking about it or experiencing feelings about it. Sometimes teens may bury their feelings so deeply that they really believe they have no emotional response to the event.

What do you do

when you experience strong emotions? Are you comfortable expressing them, or do you keep them to yourself?

But we all do have strong emotions like sadness, anxiety, anger, and guilt after a crisis situation. People who seem to have little response to a disturbing event are actually suppressing their emotions. Burying emotions does not make you feel normal, like nothing has happened. Instead, you may feel strangely shut down, numb, and empty. It is normal and common to feel shut off from your emotions for a short time after a crisis event, but if you turn off your emotions for an extended time, you prevent yourself from facing and working through them. Recognizing your feelings, which will be discussed in chapters 4 and 5, enables you to move past the "chill" towards releasing your emotions and "letting go."

Thoughts in times of crisis

Crisis events affect thoughts as well as feelings. First, the physical and emotional responses take so much energy that people often find it hard to concentrate on anything. They also commonly find it hard to make decisions. They generally feel like they can't think straight. This can be disturbing and may impair one's abilities at school or at work, but it is normal and subsides as the crisis is resolved.

Further, after a very stressful event, many people keep replaying the incident in their minds, vividly recalling the most intense moments. Although this response can be very upsetting, it is also normal for a time and usually stops a month or so after the crisis.

On a deep level, a crisis disrupts your basic mental picture of the world. A very distressing event—a disaster, an assault, a death in the family—challenges your belief that your world is safe and reliable. A crisis is very hard for your mind to process.

Usually, with time, when you see that nothing else terrible happens, you regain confidence that your world is basically stable and trustworthy, putting the event in perspective. You recognize that the crisis is a particular incident, not something you will find everywhere. But for some time, while you feel unresolved about the crisis, your beliefs about the world are challenged. Your mind's reaction to the event combines with your physical fight or flight response and your emotions of anxiety, sadness, anger, and guilt, creating a difficult state that takes time to heal.

Behavior in times of crisis

In the aftermath of a crisis, people's difficult thoughts and feelings are often reflected in their behavior. Many teens, for example, develop problems at school, struggling with or blowing off assignments or skipping classes. Feeling on edge, they may also argue or fight with others

You may notice that your behavior changes after you experience a crisis. Some teens find it difficult to keep up with their classes, or may withdraw from their friends.

more than they used to. Further, after experiencing a crisis, many people withdraw from others, keeping to themselves. They may be so sad, angry, anxious, or mistrustful that they have a hard time connecting with others.

Another common behavior is trying to avoid places and situations that remind you of the crisis. The incident was so stressful that you may try to stay away from anything that might bring back the feelings you experienced. For instance, a young man who was mugged in a park at night might not only avoid parks, but also stop going out at night, or even avoid going any place altogether where he might encounter strangers.

Similarly, people may become preoccupied with checking their environment to try to ensure that nothing dangerous will happen again. They may double-check window and door locks, look out with extra alertness for fire hazards, or keep very close tabs on the people close to them.

An especially negative reaction to a crisis situation is abusing drugs or alcohol. Often when people are under great stress, they are tempted to use drugs or alcohol to escape their tough feelings. It is much better not to. Drugs and alcohol may make you feel better for a moment, but in the long term they make your brain chemistry more depressed, cloudy, and anxious. These effects of drugs and alcohol make it even harder to heal from a crisis.

All of the behaviors described here are common responses to a crisis. But people who bury their feelings after a crisis are especially likely to have trouble with their behavior. Ignoring or hiding your feelings does not make them go away. Instead, your emotions come out in behavior, like poor school performance, withdrawal, fighting, or drug and alcohol abuse. Burying feelings after a crisis may also lead to mental health problems like depression and anxiety disorders.

It is important to realize that we all have tough feelings in the aftermath of a crisis. When we recognize our feelings and thoughts, they no longer rule our behavior; we can address them directly and resolve them, instead of just acting them out.

In contrast, the more we try to shut out our reaction to a crisis, the harder it is to heal from it. Troubling thoughts, feelings, and behaviors are normal after a crisis, but if they go on for a long time or seem too overwhelming, you may have depression or an anxiety disorder and need to seek professional counseling.

Depression and Anxiety

Danielle has been struggling for so long that she feels like she's at the end of her rope. She's nervous all the time, and is always worried that the worst will happen. Sometimes she's so exhausted from worrying that all she wants to do is stay in bed. "Why bother even getting up?" she thinks to herself. At times she's so down that it's hard for her to think of anything really good in her life. And talking to people seems like an effort that's more than she can handle.

Recently Danielle's dad left a brochure on the kitchen counter about common mental health disorders. After reading it, Danielle wondered if maybe she had depression or an anxiety disorder. Now she's thinking of calling a clinic for help. "Maybe," she thinks, "I can get relief after all."

Everyone who experiences a very stressful event faces difficult emotions, but most people resolve their feelings over time. However, some people find that their feelings become particularly overwhelming, especially when they do not get support from others. Some may develop mental health problems like clinical depression (feelings of sadness and a loss of interest in activities that lasts for a long time), or an anxiety disorder (feelings of nervousness that do not go away and interfere with daily life).

Clinical depression and anxiety disorders sometimes also occur to people who did not experience a recent trauma. Sometimes these mental health problems are caused by lingering feelings from stressful events in the past, feelings that are not yet resolved. Depression and anxiety can also stem from biological causes. For

Depression and anxiety are strong emotions that are difficult to resolve on your own. Although you may be tempted to withdraw from your loved ones when you are feeling anxious or sad, you should accept their support if your feelings become overwhelming after a crisis.

instance, some people have too little of certain natural chemicals like **serotonin**, which affects the brain's ability to process emotions. Some may have too much of other chemicals, like **adrenalin**, which produces the body's fight or flight response. Further, some health conditions, like low blood sugar, and some medications, like birth control pills, can cause feelings of depression or anxiety.

Whatever the cause, severe problems with anxiety or depression are a kind of crisis, just as stressful events like the death of a loved one, crime, and disasters are. Some people find it easier to identify a stressful event in the outside world—a fire or a robbery, for example—than a problem with their mental health. It is important to understand that clinical depression and anxiety disorders are real, serious problems.

Some people who suffer from depression or anxiety disorders are reluctant to get help. They may believe that they are at fault for having the disorder, and that they should just get over it. In fact, clinical depression and anxiety disorders are health conditions. Like a broken leg or pneumonia, a mental illness is not the fault of the person who suffers from it, and it requires proper treatment. Just as you turn to a doctor to heal a broken leg, or the fire department to put out a fire, you can turn to mental health practitioners to treat clinical depression and anxiety disorders.

Symptoms

The terms depression and anxiety are probably familiar to you. We commonly use the word depressed to mean feeling sad or down, and the word anxious to mean nervous. It is normal to have these feelings for limited periods of time, especially when you are under stress. The feelings may indicate mental health problems, called clinical depression or anxiety disorder, only when they last for a long time (more than a few weeks) and are so troublesome that they interfere with your daily life on a regular basis.

The following are the primary symptoms of clinical depression, and you may be suffering from this mental health disorder if these symptoms last for an extended period of time: feelings of sadness, hopelessness, worthlessness; difficulty concentrating; lack of interest in things you used to enjoy; loss of appetite or overeating; stomachaches; problems with sleep; lack of

What would you do if you experienced many of the symptoms of anxiety or depression after a crisis?

energy; a sense that your life is overwhelming; thoughts of harming yourself or committing suicide.

If you have thoughts of hurting yourself or committing suicide, it is urgent that you seek help immediately. Most people who consider suicide don't truly want to die; what they really want is relief from their painful feelings, but they can't see any way to feel better. Be aware that professional help is available, and it does work. Mental health practitioners are specially trained to find ways of bringing you relief. Talk to someone at a mental health clinic or a suicide hotline (found in the Yellow Pages); in an emergency, call 911 or go to the emergency room of your local hospital.

The major symptoms of anxiety disorders include some or all of the following, experienced for an extended period of time: intense worrying; nervousness; a sense that danger is lurking; difficulty concentrating; restlessness; shortness of breath; neck and back aches; stomachaches; poor appetite or overeating; problems with sleep.

Post-traumatic stress disorder (PTSD) is a particular kind of anxiety disorder that sometimes occurs after a traumatic event. You might have PTSD if you experience several of the following symptoms for an extended period of time: nightmares; replaying the traumatic event in your mind and feeling unable to stop the memories; avoiding things or places that might trigger memories of the event; feeling easily alarmed or on edge; feeling that danger is lurking; difficulty concentrating; problems with sleep. These symptoms are normal for a short time after a stressful event, but they may indicate PTSD if they last for more than a month.

Thoughts

Anxiety disorders and clinical depression are usually characterized by certain kinds of thoughts, as well as feelings. People who have anxiety or depression tend to focus

Negative thoughts usually accompany anxiety disorders and depression, and these thoughts can make everyday tasks like homework and school especially difficult. However, keep in mind that experiencing one crisis does not necessarily mean that bad things will always happen to you.

on negative aspects of their lives rather than positive ones. Distressing events loom so largely in their minds that they overlook the pleasurable things in their lives. For instance, a girl who is mourning the death of her grandfather might feel very sensitive to other upsetting incidents—a low grade on a test, a rude remark from a kid at school. She may be so overwhelmed that she forgets about the positive events in her life—her close relationship with her sister, her great grade on a term paper. Her thought pattern is completely normal during a time of mourning, but if it continues for a very long time, she may be seriously depressed or anxious.

A similar kind of thought common to people with depression is the belief that one negative event is part of a general pattern of negative events. Similarly, a person with an anxiety disorder feels that when one frightening event has occurred, more frightening events are likely to occur around every corner. For instance, a boy whose parents are divorced might think that no relationship ever succeeds and that he cannot count on any relationship to last. A boy who thinks this way is likely to suffer from severe depression or anxiety.

Often people who have anxiety or depression also

believe they hold more responsibility for events than they really do. For instance, children of substance abusers commonly think they are responsible for their parents' drug or alcohol abuse. In fact, children have no control over their parents' substance abuse and are in no way to blame for it. As kids feel they should somehow stop their parents' drug or alcohol use, something they have no control over, they may feel severely anxious or depressed.

Coping

Many people experience clinical depression and anxiety disorders, but most people who get help recover very well. The first step in coping with clinical depression or an anxiety disorder is realizing that you have a mental health condition. If you recognize that your painful feelings and thoughts are the symptoms of an illness, you can get treatment for it. You do not have to suffer! You can cope with and recover from anxiety and depression.

When you discover that you have clinical depression or an anxiety disorder, you should try to understand that your mental health condition, like any illness, is not your fault. Just as people who have asthma, for example, generally do not blame themselves for their illness, you can be assured that you are not to blame for your depression or anxiety disorder. The roots of mental health problems are stressful events and/or brain chemistry, not personal inadequacy. Rather than blaming yourself for feeling bad, you need to seek treatment for your condition.

How would you feel

if your friend was suffering from depression? Would your feelings be different if she had a broken leg?

Depression and anxiety feel overwhelming and never-ending. People with clinical depression feel like a dark cloud hangs over everything in their lives. People with an anxiety disorder often feel that their nervousness can never go away. Thus, sufferers of depression or anxiety may find it hard to believe that they can ever get relief. It is important to understand that these doubts about feeling better are caused by the cloud of depression or anxiety. Try to understand that, in fact, relief is available.

In order to get relief from depression or anxiety, practice the coping skills we will discuss in chapters 4, 5, and 6. As these chapters explain, it is helpful to eat well and exercise regularly, get proper sleep, practice relaxation techniques, appreciate the positive aspects of your life, and avoid blaming yourself for things you are not responsible for.

Most important of all, you can help yourself by turning to others. Tell someone you trust that you believe you may have clinical depression or an anxiety disorder and ask him or her for help. You can talk to your parents, another adult relative, a close friend, a teacher, a school counselor, or a religious cleric. Sharing your feelings with others helps you put your emotions in perspective and enables you to receive the support and encouragement that everyone needs in difficult times. Further, adults can help you find professional treatment that meets your needs.

Professional help

If you suspect that you have clinical depression or an anxiety disorder, you need to see a mental health professional. If you wish, you can visit a family care physician to see if you have any physical conditions that are contributing to your emotional difficulties. A family doctor can also refer you to a mental health practitioner. Mental health practitioners include psychiatrists, psychologists, and clinical social workers. They are specially trained to diagnose mental health problems and are expert at finding ways to bring you relief. They will probably also check into your physical health.

Sharing your thoughts and feelings with someone you trust after a crisis is an important step in healing. Parents, teachers, and friends can help you keep the crisis in perspective, and offer you good advice about resolving any negative feelings you may have.

You can find a health or mental health practitioner in the Yellow Pages, or by asking your parents, teacher, school counselor, or school nurse. If cost is a concern, you can ask your parents if they can pay for treatment or if they have insurance that covers the fees. Alternatively, you can look for a community health or mental health clinic, which provides service for low cost. If you need immediate assistance, twenty-four-hour-a-day mental health crisis hotlines (listed in the Yellow Pages) have trained staff that provide guidance and referrals. The treatment for depression and anxiety disorders is highly effective, but you need to take the first step and seek help.

Recognizing
Your Feelings

■ Jason's parents have separated and will be getting divorced soon. He knows that they were fighting a lot and that it is best for them to live apart. Plus his friends have divorced parents, so he thinks it shouldn't be a big deal. The only problem is he's been having so many stomach aches. The doctor can't find anything wrong with his stomach, but it keeps him up at night. During the day, he feels run down, and he can't seem to feel interested in playing basketball or running around with his friends after school like he used to. And he keeps getting mad at people for the dumbest things. Everyone seems to annoy him.

Sometimes people, especially kids, who experience a crisis don't realize how strongly it affects them. Like Jason, they may think the situation is no big deal, so they are confused by their troubled feelings or behavior. It is important to acknowledge that a very disruptive situation creates serious physical, emotional, and mental responses. A major

Sometimes it may difficult to identify your feelings after a crisis if you don't realize how serious a situation is. Even if you feel like the crisis you experienced is fairly common, like your parents' divorce, do not dismiss your feelings. What really matters is how the crisis affects you.

loss, assault, disaster, or mental health condition is indeed a big deal.

A key first step to healing a strain is recognizing your feelings and their source. Whenever you show signs of great strain, you need to try to figure out what might be causing you stress and pay close attention to how you are feeling.

Awareness

When you are aware of your emotions, you can address them directly instead of expressing them inaccurately. For example, in a time of crisis people often have physical problems, like stomachaches, headaches, or muscle pains, that are caused by stress; they can clear up their ailments only if they address their feelings of stress. Or people might lash out with anger at others when they are really angry about a disturbing event. Fighting an innocent target will not help you resolve your anger; you can only resolve your feelings once you realize what you are actually mad about.

Sometimes people also get down on themselves when they are actually upset about a situation that is not their fault. For instance, a boy who has trouble concentrating at school after he's faced a disaster may think he's just bad at his classes. Instead, he needs to realize that he's having difficulty focusing because he's upset about the crisis event, not because he's unintelligent. Recognizing how you feel about a crisis keeps you from blaming your troubled responses on yourself.

> **How do you feel**
>
> **when something bad happens to you? Do you immediately blame your self, or realize that the situation may have been beyond your control?**

Becoming aware of your feelings about a crisis is an important first step to taking action to resolve them. In addition, sometimes just identifying your emotions is already enough to lighten and defuse them. Naming a feeling gives you distance from it, making it a little less overwhelming. If you say, "I'm sad," you feel a bit more in control than if you were just suffused with gloom without being conscious of it. You can also then decide how you want to handle your sadness.

Further, identifying your feelings puts limits on them. You realize that this is how you feel now in this particular situation, rather than believing your feelings are permanent and apply to all situations. For example, you may see that you are fearful about a disturbing situation you have experienced like an earthquake, a violent crime, or the instability of an alcoholic parent; realizing this, you can understand that your anxiety lies in that one situation, instead of worrying that danger lies everywhere. Or you may become aware that you are sad about an event like the death of your cousin or your family's move after a fire, or that you are sad because you have clinical depression; you can then understand that your sadness is rooted in a particular circumstance, rather than feeling that life is miserable altogether.

Obstacles

Often in a time of crisis, people don't want to become aware of their troubled feelings. They may believe it is wrong to be upset because it is irrational. For instance, after the death of a loved one, a boy might think, "death is a natural part of life, so why get anxious about it?" Or a girl whose family survived a tornado might think, "we're all safe, so there's nothing to be upset about." It is important to realize that feelings are not always logical.

Sometimes people also shut out their feelings because they think their sadness, fear, or anger is immature or weak. They think being strong means not letting events get to you, but actually, facing your emotions is brave. People may also fear that paying attention to their feelings is selfish. They think of other people who have it worse. But each of us is equally important.

Facing your feelings in a time of crisis can be hard. You may think if you ignore your troubled emotions and thoughts, they'll go away and you'll never have to deal with

Ignoring your feelings instead of expressing them after a crisis is an obstacle to resolving your emotions. Suppressing your emotions will separate you from your friends and loved ones.

them. Further, you may have buried your response to a crisis so strongly that you don't even know how you feel about the situation. You may really believe you don't have any response to it.

Numbness is normal for a time after a fight or flight response to stress, as described in chapter 2. But when your feelings are buried for a long time, you run a high risk of developing serious problems. Wishing away emotions doesn't work. Instead, they come out in disguised forms, like getting ill, fighting with others, or developing severe mental health conditions like depression or an anxiety disorder. Ignoring your emotions in a time of a crisis only prolongs them and makes them harder to heal.

How to recognize your feelings

To face your feelings during a time of crisis, you need first to find a safe, relaxing environment. If there are serious conflicts in your family, go outside; if being in public makes you nervous, go someplace private. In a tense environment, you face too much stress to handle looking inward. Find a place where you feel protected. Sometimes just becoming more relaxed is enough to enable your emotions to float to the surface, where you can examine them.

Where would you go

if you needed a quiet place to examine your thoughts and feelings?

Try asking yourself how you feel in response to the crisis you've experienced. If you come up empty or don't know how you feel, you can ask yourself more specific questions. First, it is often helpful to focus on your bodily sensations, as they provide clues to your emotions. Fatigue, shallow breathing, headaches, stomachaches, or back pains are common signs of tension from fight or flight feelings. Second, see if you are experiencing any of the common emotions described in chapter 2. Do you feel angry, sad, nervous, scared, guilty, or ashamed? If so, can you see how these feelings stem from the stress you've endured?

Try to notice your feelings without judging them or yourself. Remember that your emotions are normal responses to a situation that was out of your hands, and that you are safe now, while acknowledging that your feelings are real.

Many people find that writing in a private notebook or journal or talking into a tape recorder is very helpful to air their feelings. Getting concerns out in words helps to release them. If you write or speak freely and openly, you may discover thoughts and feelings you didn't realize you

Writing down your thoughts and feelings in a journal or letter can help you express emotions that you may not be comfortable speaking out loud.

had. Reflecting in words can also give you perspective and insight on your emotions.

Similarly, you may find it useful to write a letter to someone, a letter that you will not send. Perhaps there is someone you wish you could talk to but he or she is not in your life. Or maybe you would find it helpful to get things off your chest to someone you know, but you're too afraid of how he or she would react. Address a letter to the person and write everything you'd like to say. Imagining that you're expressing yourself to someone else may help you face, understand, and release your concerns.

Making art is another excellent way to face your feelings. Try drawing, painting, or sculpting whatever images come to mind, rather than trying to copy an image or object. Making art in this way helps you discover and release your emotions. It helps you gain perspective and empowerment by giving your feelings form. The process may be so absorbing that it frees you from the tension you have been bearing, allowing you to relax in your inner mind and imagination.

Sharing Your Thoughts and Feelings

■ The most frightening day of Lauren's life was the day she came home from school and found out her dad had a heart attack. He made a full recovery, but she worried about it a lot afterward. At first she didn't want to talk to her parents about how nervous she was. "They have enough to deal with," she thought, "and I don't want to be selfish."

But her dad convinced her to open up to him, and it helped so much. He explained what was wrong with his health and how he and the doctors had the problem under control. Lauren also realized that she was worried she hadn't been nice enough to him before the heart attack, and that she'd been walking on eggshells around him ever since. But her dad reassured her that what makes him feel best is her just being herself.

Sometimes people who experience a crisis are reluctant to share their thoughts and feelings with others. They may close themselves off from the people around them. But no one

Some people may worry that talking about their thoughts and feelings is a sign of weakness or immaturity. However, learning to communicate with your friends and family to ask for help and guidance when you need it is a sign of maturity.

can cope with a crisis alone. We all need to turn to others in hard times. As many studies have shown, we heal from a crisis much more easily when we share our concerns with people we trust.

Communication

Expressing your thoughts and feelings to people you trust helps you in many ways. First, communicating helps you sort out the turbulent emotions and thoughts running through you. It enables you to identify your feelings, keeping them from being an overwhelming jumble.

Just putting your feelings into words that someone else hears and understands makes them seem more manageable. And discussing your concerns with others can give you insight and perspective. When you can understand your feelings and where they come from, you can deal with them more easily.

Further, sharing your thoughts and feelings enables others to actively help you. It allows people who care about you to give you encouragement and reassurance, as well as useful advice and practical aid. Adults can also give you invaluable information.

Finding out the facts from adults can be very important in a time of crisis. When you don't know the facts, you tend to worry about frightening scenarios that aren't true. It is easier to cope when you know exactly what you are facing. For instance, in the aftermath of a terrorist bombing, knowledgeable adults can explain to you what the risks are of further attacks and what steps are being taken to prevent them. This helps you to hold a rational perspective on the event, rather than fearing widespread dangers that are in fact unlikely to happen.

Similarly, if your parents are divorcing, you can talk with them about visitation arrangements with the parent who has left the home. They can also explain to you any changes in your family's financial picture. Getting a clear, accurate picture of your family's circumstances helps you adjust and keeps you from having false fears. Your

> **How would you feel**
>
> **if your parents were getting divorced? What questions would you ask them about your family's future?**

parents can also discuss with you their reasons for separating, helping you to see that it had nothing to do with you. They can reassure you that the divorce has no effect on their love and support of you.

Adults can also give you practical help when you share your troubles with them. For instance, crime victims can get adults' help in reporting the crime to the authorities, getting medical attention, and taking steps to feel more secure in the future. Adults are available to help you in many practical ways, more than you often realize. For instance, many young people in a crisis do not realize that teachers and parents are usually willing to reduce kids' responsibilities while they are recovering. If you tell your teacher or parents about your troubles following a crisis, you can discuss getting extra time for assignments, limiting your household chores, or other ways to lighten your load for a while. It is much better to discuss lightening your responsibilities than to risk getting overwhelmed by them.

Finally, sharing your thoughts and feelings about a crisis with people you trust lets you feel more connected with them. Relationships of caring and trust give you comfort, nourishment, and strength at a time when you need it most. When you let others know how you're feeling, you can receive the consideration and compassion you deserve. Knowing that you matter to people and that people stand behind you helps a great deal.

Obstacles

Despite all the clear benefits of sharing thoughts and feelings, some people believe that communicating won't help them. Often people don't want to share their concerns with others because they think it is weak to need other people. They may think they're strong enough to handle their problems on their own. But a crisis is too hard for anyone to handle by themselves. Everyone needs a shoulder to lean on during very tough times. It is a sign of strength to ask for the help you need.

People who don't get support during times of crisis

Attempting to handle your emotions by yourself after a crisis is not always the best approach, as it may hinder your recovery and open the door to other serious problems like depression, anxiety, and substance abuse.

usually have more difficulty recovering. They are more likely to develop mental health conditions and problems like substance abuse, fighting, and difficulties forming satisfying relationships. When you don't share your negative emotions in a time of crisis, they may take root inside you and become much harder to release.

You may fear that other people will judge your feelings or thoughts badly, perhaps thinking your concerns are stupid, babyish, or selfish. But it is normal to have tough, irrational feelings during a time of crisis, and everyone has such feelings at one time or other. A compassionate person does not think less of you when you share your concerns, but rather feels closer to you.

You may also find it hard to believe that people will understand your thoughts and feelings or that they will even care about your problems. During a time of crisis, your trust in the world has been disrupted. It is important to try to repair your trust. Someone out there does care about you and can understand you. You need only to make an effort to open up to him or her.

Family violence and abuse

Children whose parents abuse drugs or alcohol or are violent have an especially hard time opening up to others. They cannot turn safely to their parents because their parents are the problem. They need to tell someone outside the family about the abuse. Substance abusers often deny that they have a problem. Thus their children often hesitate to admit the problem too. Indeed, kids often feel that they are responsible for their parents' substance abuse, believing that if only they behave properly they can make their parents stop. If your parent abuses drugs or alcohol it is important to realize that your parent is responsible for it, not you. Nothing you do can make your parents use drugs or alcohol and nothing you do can make them stop.

> **What would you do**
>
> **if your mom or dad was abusing drugs or acting violently?**

You need to recognize that you have a serious family problem and take care of yourself by turning to others. Look up or ask a school counselor about Alateen, a group for teens whose parents have drug or alcohol problems, or Nar-Anon, which helps kids whose parents abuse drugs. You can also find a social worker or psychologist to talk to.

Similarly, children who are the victims of family violence often fear telling others because they love their parents; they may not want to admit that their parents have a problem and they may fear getting their parents into trouble by telling. Children of abusive parents also commonly believe they are responsible for their own mistreatment. But you never deserve abuse, even if you misbehave. If your parent is violent, it is very important to recognize that he or she has a serious, dangerous problem that requires professional help. If you tell someone about the problem, your whole family can get help, including your abusive parent.

Turn to an adult you know and trust to help you, look in the phone book for a mental health center or community health clinic, or call the National Domestic Violence Hotline, toll-free, at 1-800-799-SAFE (7233). If you find that anyone in your family is in immediate danger, leave the house right away, call 911, and tell the emergency operator your address and what is happening.

Choosing helpful listeners

Whatever crisis you experience, you need to choose people to talk to who are helpful listeners. Helpful listeners hear what you are saying without judging or criticizing you. They respect you and try to understand your point of view and circumstances. They can focus on your needs and concerns and place importance on them.

Unfortunately, some people do not respond well to hearing about others' troubles. These people may dismiss your feelings of crisis, saying "It's no big deal, just forget about it." They may say you are wrong to have feelings like anger, sadness, guilt, or anxiety. "You shouldn't feel that way," they might tell you, or, "Stop feeling that way and just put it behind you."

Do you know

a helpful listener with whom you can share your thoughts and feelings?

If someone denies or discounts your feelings, remember

that it is perfectly normal to have tough emotions in a time of crisis, and that trying to block them out only makes you feel worse. Be assured that you are entitled to your feelings and need to express them openly. You can try explaining to the person that you need someone to listen to you and understand you. Or you can simply look elsewhere for a more helpful listener.

You can try talking to a relative, a friend, a teacher, a school counselor, a coach, or a clergy member—anyone you trust to help you. Sometimes teens are reluctant to tell their parents about their troubles. If your parents are abusive, you are right to turn elsewhere. But otherwise, consider talking to your parents. They can be your best source of support.

You may fear that your parents won't understand you, will be too pushy about telling you what to do, or be disappointed in you for being so troubled. If your crisis is your parents' divorce or illness, you may fear that they are too absorbed with their own problems to deal with yours, or that they'll get mad or hurt if you tell them how badly you're feeling.

But parents are usually far more understanding, sympathetic, and supportive than many teens give them credit for. Most parents place their highest priority on their children's well-being. They want to know how you are feeling and give you the attention and help you need. They can offer you the benefits of their experience, maturity, and resources at a time when you most need support. Even just getting reassurance that your parents are behind you can make you feel a lot better.

Professional help

Many people also find it useful to talk with a professional counselor. You need to seek counseling if you suspect you have a mental health problem (if your emotions

If you think you may be suffering from a mental health condition like anxiety or depression, it may be time to seek professional help from a school counselor or a doctor. These conditions can cause problems like fatigue and difficulty concentrating in school.

feel overwhelming and interfere with your daily life for an extended period), if your parents abuse drugs or alcohol or are violent, or if you have been raped. These crises are too difficult to handle without professional care. But counseling can also help in any tough time, giving you extra help in coping and healing.

Psychiatrists, psychologists, and clinical social workers are specially trained to listen and understand people. They are expert in finding ways to relieve your troubled feelings and help you resolve your problems. In addition to talking with you, they may recommend medication that can help you recover.

Some mental health professionals also run **support groups**. In these groups, people who all have the same problem talk with each other. The groups can offer you perspective, understanding, and encouragement.

To find a professional counselor or support group, you can look in the Yellow Pages or ask a doctor, school nurse, or guidance counselor for recommendations. The staff at mental health hotlines (found in the Yellow Pages) can also give you a referral. A hotline, in addition, can give you immediate assistance if you feel you need urgent help.

If you choose to seek counseling, be sure to find a practitioner or group you feel comfortable with. If you don't like one, you can always find another. Further, if you are worried about cost, you can select a counselor that is covered by your parents' health insurance, or look for a mental health clinic or social service agency that offers care for free or low charge.

Coping

■ When Stephanie's best friend Kim died of cancer last year, she was flooded with pain. The loss hurt her deeply, and made her angry about how unfair life could be. After the funeral, she knew she had to go on with her life, but how? Talking with her mom helped her understand the normal feelings of grief and gave her suggestions on coping with them. Week by week, month by month, she gradually grew stronger. She started to spend more time with another friend and grew closer to her.

Now Stephanie finds that she's not thinking about Kim's illness and death as much. She'll never forget or stop loving Kim, but she sees her friend as a cherished memory. She can finally remember Kim without feeling pain. She feels whole again, and finds that she actually feels good about herself, her life, and her future.

Difficult feelings and thoughts are natural during a time of crisis, but you can find ways to cope with them and resolve them. Nearly everyone suffers a crisis at one time or

An important part of coping with a crisis is sharing your thoughts and feelings with others. It is also essential that you take good care of yourself physically by eating right, exercising, and getting enough sleep.

other, but most people recover well. Human beings have great capacities to heal from emotional stresses, just as they can heal from physical injuries like fractured limbs. And learning that you can surmount a crisis can help you feel more empowered for the rest of your life.

How to cope—the basics

In a time of great strain, you need to take extra good care of yourself, with kindness, compassion, and patience. First, as we have seen, an important step in coping is recognizing your feelings and thoughts and getting support from others. Remember that your troubled feelings are normal during a time of crisis, so don't get down on yourself for having them. Instead, pay close attention to your feelings and share them with others.

Note that if you live in a household where there is family violence, you must recognize that you are living in a crisis situation and turn to others to take steps to ensure your physical safety. You must be physically safe before you can heal the emotional effects of the crisis you have endured.

In the aftermath of any crisis event, be sure to take special care of your most basic needs. Try to eat nutritiously, exercise, and get adequate sleep to support your health. Neglecting your health will only make things harder. Plus, studies have shown that healthy nutrition, sufficient sleep, and exercise help relieve emotional stress.

Try to have regular, balanced meals with plenty of fruits and vegetables, and avoid junk foods like fast food, sweets, and chips if you can. You may find it hard to eat well at this time; don't stress about it, but eat as best as you can. In addition, avoid alcohol and drugs, including caffeine (found in coffee, tea, and colas). Overall, these chemicals will likely cause you to feel more depressed or anxious.

If you have trouble sleeping, try drinking warm milk or herbal tea, or taking a warm bath before bed. In times of crisis, many people sleep better with a night light in their room. Getting regular exercise also helps you sleep better.

Exercising during a tough time can be hard, as stress commonly makes people feel tired. But exercise releases natural chemicals, called **endorphins**, that lift your spirits. It is also a great way to release feelings of anger. Try walking briskly, running, bicycling, swimming, or playing sports. Dancing also gives you a good workout.

Another basic need is managing your schoolwork. Falling behind at school will only add to your troubles. For some kids, schoolwork is a good distraction from their worries. But remember that if you have difficulty concentrating, let your teachers or guidance counselor know what is going on and ask them for help. They can give you extra leeway during this hard time.

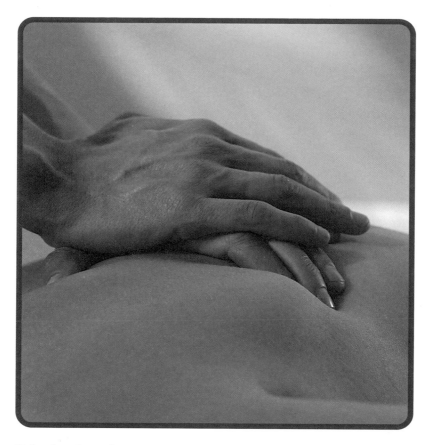

Relaxing through massage, a warm bath, or an activity that helps you deal with stress are great ways to cope with the anxiety that may follow a crisis.

Relaxation

Another important way to cope is getting yourself to relax physically and mentally. Relaxation helps your body to calm down from fight or flight chemicals and helps your mind and emotions become more centered and balanced. Give yourself a time out each day from stimulating media like TV, fast music, and video games. Instead, try massaging your scalp, neck, upper back, and shoulders, or ask a friend or relative to do it. Soak in a warm tub, pet your cat or dog, walk in a park, or sit in the sun—whatever makes you feel relaxed.

You can also try relaxation techniques like focused breathing. Take five minutes for yourself, close your eyes, and breathe deeply, taking full inhalations and exhalations. Just focus on the natural sensations of your breath and let other thoughts drift away. Or try muscle relaxation: lie very still, close your eyes, breathe, and direct each part of your body to relax, beginning with your feet and moving up to your face. You might also try to visualize a soothing image, like waves lapping a shore or a peaceful meadow. Let yourself rest in the feeling of calm for a while.

A positive mental outlook

It's important to air your feelings in a time of crisis, but it's also helpful to use positive thoughts to keep your distress in perspective. You can try to keep a positive mental outlook even though you know that it's natural to be upset at this time. For example, you can remind yourself that you've overcome tough situations in the past; if you could surmount those hard situations, you can handle this one too. Try too to remember the good things in your life, the things you are grateful for. Some people also find that religious prayer helps them feel comforted and hopeful.

> **Can you describe** a crisis that you handled well, and what you did to cope with your thoughts and feelings?

Moreover, try to understand the crisis accurately. As discussed throughout this book, tough times are easier to handle when you know what you're dealing with. Reading and asking adults about the crisis and its common emotional effects helps you clear up concerns and confusion. Further, bear in mind that feelings are often irrational. For instance, as we have seen, it is common to feel that a crisis event is your fault when in fact you are not at all responsible for it. And after a crisis, people often fear that other disruptive events will happen, even though in reality they are unlikely to occur. It's helpful to both recognize your feelings and keep them in rational perspective.

Lightening your mood

In the aftermath of a crisis, you may not feel like having fun, or it may seem strange to you to consider having a good time. But distracting yourself from your troubles and lightening your mood sometimes can help you cope. You need to face your emotional response to the crisis in order to process and release it, but you also need to replenish your strength, to recharge your battery.

You can try escaping into an enjoyable book, TV program, or video. Going to the movies can be an excellent break from your troubles; it's hard to think about anything else at the movie theater. Other possibilities include listening to fun music, dancing, playing with your pet, making art or crafts, going to a museum, or buying yourself clothes you really like. Doing something absorbing and pleasant can be very nourishing, even if it doesn't make your problems go away. Try what feels right for you.

Social activities are especially important in a time of crisis. In tough times, many people tend to withdraw from others, but actually, spending some time with other people helps you regain a sense of trust, confidence, and normality. Spend time with friends doing something fun or just hanging out. Try joining a club or getting involved in an extra-curricular school activity that sounds enjoyable. After a crisis, many people find it helpful to volunteer at a service program or organization, like a senior center, a program that teaches people to read, an animal shelter, or a food drive for the hungry. Volunteering not only occupies your mind and gives you contact with friendly people, it also gives you the empowerment of helping others.

After-school activities like sports and clubs can help you rebuild confidence and improve your mood after a crisis. Similarly, volunteering to help the less fortunate can give you a sense of accomplishment, and help you keep your own problems in perspective.

Acceptance

No matter how much you use coping skills when you are under great strain, you will likely still have upsetting feelings during this time. Difficult emotions are normal and natural during a time of crisis. It is important to accept that you are going through a crisis and that you have tough feelings. You can't wish your emotions away, so it's healthy to accept that this a hard period. Don't hesitate to reach out and talk to people you trust and lean on them for support. Remember too that professional help is always available if you need it.

Be patient and remember that you won't feel bad forever. It takes time to absorb the stressful event, process it, and heal, but you can definitely recover, just as your body can recover from a wound. Be gentle with yourself, and try to take each day and week one at a time. Practice coping skills to help yourself along. When you take care of yourself, with time your painful emotions will gradually resolve themselves and pass. You will regain your sense of safety and stability, and the crisis will become part of your past.

Surviving a crisis can bring you positive gains, difficult though the experience is. It can deepen your understanding of life's challenges and show you that you have the strength to endure and overcome them. It enables you to learn coping skills that you can apply to any stresses you encounter in the future. And reaching out to others in a tough time can bring you closer to them, giving you enriched relationships of caring, trust, and open communication.

To learn more about crises, their effects on feelings and thoughts, and ways of coping, see the resources listed at the end of this book. Be sure also to seek out people you trust with whom to share your own feelings, thoughts, and experiences.

Glossary

Adrenalin – a chemical substance secreted by the adrenal gland that triggers responses like the fight or flight reaction.

Anxiety – a sense of nervousness or fear that is normal during times of crisis, but that can become a problem if it interferes with daily life.

Crisis – a difficult and disruptive situation, like a divorce or death of a loved one.

Depression – a mood or emotional state marked by sadness, inactivity, and an inability to enjoy life.

Endorphins – natural chemicals released by the brain that elevate your mood.

Fight or flight response – a biological response to an emergency that prepares the body to fight a predator or flee a dangerous situation.

Grief – a set of reactions someone experiences after a crisis or important loss, which include strong emotions like sadness and physical symptoms like stomachaches and fatigue.

Post-traumatic stress disorder – an anxiety disorder that causes the sufferer to relive a trauma, to avoid situations similar to that trauma, and to be anxious and expectant of future traumatic events.

Serotonin – a chemical messenger in the brain that affects the brain's ability to process emotions.

Support groups – groups of people who gather together to discuss their thoughts and feelings about a particular crisis they have in common, such as a mental health problem.

Further Reading

Books:

Cobain, Bev. *When Nothing Matters Anymore: A Survival Guide for Depressed Teens*. Minneapolis: Free Spirit, 1998.

Fitzgerald, Helen. *The Grieving Teen: A Guide for Teenagers and Their Friends*. New York: Simon & Schuster, 2000.

Maloney, Michael and Rachel Kranz. *Straight Talk about Anxiety and Depression*. New York: Dell, 1991.

Palmer, Jed. *Everything You Need to Know When You Are a Victim of a Violent Crime*. New York: Rosen Publishing Group, 1994.

Porterfield, Kay Marie. *Straight Talk about Post-Traumatic Stress Disorder*. New York: Facts on File, 1996.

Rench, Janice E. *Family Violence: How to Recognize and Survive It*. Minneapolis: Lerner, 1992.

Wagner, Heather Lehr. *Understanding and Coping with Divorce*. Philadelphia: Chelsea House, 2002.

Websites:

American Psychological Association. *helping.apa.org*

Mental Help Net. *www.mentalhelp.net*

National Mental Health Association Resource Center. *www.nmha.org/infoctr*

Hotlines:

National Domestic Violence Hotline.
1-800-799-SAFE (1-800-799-7233).

National Hopeline Network suicide crisis hotline.
1-800-SUICIDE (1-800-784-2433).

National Youth Crisis Hotline.
1-800-HIT-HOME (1-800-448-4663).

Index

Index

About the Author

Michele Alpern is the author of numerous works for young adults, including *The Effects of Job Loss on the Family* (Chelsea House, 2002) and *Teen Pregnancy* (Chelsea House, 2002). She received her M.A. from Columbia University and is a Ph.D. candidate at Rutgers University. She is also an artist.

About the Editor

Marvin Rosen is a licensed clinical psychologist who practices in Media, Pennsylvania. He received his doctorate degree from the University of Pennsylvania in 1961. Since 1963, he has worked with intellectually and emotionally challenged people at Elwyn, Inc. in Pennsylvania, with clinical, administrative, research, and training responsibilities. He also conducts a private practice of psychology. Dr. Rosen has taught psychology at the University of Pennsylvania, Bryn Mawr College, and West Chester University. He has written or edited seven book and numerous professional articles in the areas of psychology, rehabilitation, emotional disturbance, and mental retardation.

WITHDRAWN